I0414861

HAIKUS

OF

ALL SEASONS IX

THE HEAVENS

AND THE EARTH

MAYUMI ITOH

Copyright © Mayumi Itoh 2019

All rights reserved.

ISBN: 9781079185454

This work is subject to copyright. All rights are solely and

exclusively reserved by this author, whether the whole or

part of the material is concerned, including rights of

translation, reprinting, reuse of illustrations, recitation,

broadcasting, and reproduction in any form.

Cover design © Mayumi Itoh 2019

Front and back cover photographs: Rainbow, June 2019,

taken by the author.

In memory of

Donald Keene (1922–2019)

Contents

List of Photographs

All photographs were taken by this author, except for those credited below.

Photograph 1. The Super Blue Blood Moon—the coincidence of the largest moon of the year, the second full moon within a month, and a complete lunar eclipse, January 31, 2018, courtesy of © Morrell Chance, 2018.

Photograph 2. Nachi Great Falls, under Creative Commons license, "Nachi no taki zu" (the original painting of Nachi Great Falls before the restoration in 1985–1990), unknown painter, late 13th century, https://commons.wikimedia.org/wiki/File:Nachi_Fall_before_Restoration.jpg.

Photograph 3. "Fearfully and Wonderfully Made," after *Psalm* 139–14, acrylic painting by © Meg Itoh, 2014.

Photograph 4. Dandelion puffs.

Notes on the Text

This anthology presents each haiku in both Japanese and English so that non-Japanese-speaking readers can fully appreciate them. The text is formatted so that the first page for a given haiku (on the left side) shows the original haiku in Japanese, which is made up of a combination of Chinese characters (*kanji*) and Japanese phonetic characters (*hiragana* and *katakana*).

Then, in order to facilitate a better understanding, especially for those who are studying Japanese, the original haiku is shown in a modern spelling only in *hiragana* and *katakana*. This allows readers to see how the haiku is exactly pronounced phonetically. There are many ways to pronounce specific *kanji* words, and the original Japanese haiku does not indicate how each *kanji* character is actually pronounced. Afterward, the identification of the season word—an essential element in haiku—for the haiku is given.

On the second page for a given haiku (on the right side), a romanization of the original Japanese haiku is provided, first, so that English-speaking readers can understand how the haiku is pronounced. The words in Roman letters are divided into smaller groups of syllables, for easier reading. Then, an English translation of the haiku is presented. Due to the grammatical differences between English and Japanese, the word order of the haiku in English might be different from that of the original haiku in Japanese. It is followed by the English translation of the season word. This completes the presentation of a given haiku.

All translations, including those of haikus, were made by the author, in the form of paraphrases (not as literal translations), in order for them to make the best sense in English.

For romanizing Japanese words, the Hepburn style is primarily used, with macrons. However, macrons are not used for words known in English without macrons, as for Kyoto and Tokyo. Another exception is that "n" is not converted to "m" for words where it precedes "b, m, and p." Examples include tonbo (dragonfly), instead of tombo; sanma (Pacific saury), instead of samma; and tanpopo (dandelion), instead of tampopo. Enjoy!

Names of Japanese persons are given with the surname first, except for those who use the reversed order in English. Honorific prefixes, such as doctor and mister, are not used in the text, except in direct quotations.

Acknowledgments

I would like to thank Morrell Chance and Meg Itoh, for the loans of a photograph and a painting, and all the members of *Hoshi no shima kukai* (the Haiku Society of Star Island, a new name for the Haiku Society of New York), past and present—including but not limited to Esaka Kinuyo, Hara Yasuko, Sakuhara Aya, and Tsukino Popona—as well as Tsuneo Akaha, Kent Calder, Toshiko Calder, Morrell Chance, Steve Clemons, Akiko Collcutt, Gerald Curtis, Joshua Fogel, Hoshi Hiroshi, Ronald Hrebenar, Ellis Krauss, Mike Mochizuki, T. J. Pempel, Stephen Roddy, Gilbert Rozman, Richard Samuels, Vicki Wong, Donald Zagoria, and Quansheng Zhao, for continuous encouragement and inspirations. I extend my deep appreciation to Gregory Rewoldt and Meg Itoh for generous support.

Preface

This is the ninth haiku anthology by this author and
comprises 120 haikus, which embrace three of the seven
major themes of haiku: 1) the seasons and the weather; 2)
astronomy or the heavens; and 3) geography or the earth.
This work categorized them according to the twelve months
and the four seasons (plus the "new year" which constitutes
an independent 'season' because of its importance to
Japanese culture). This book also introduces the cultural
and historical backgrounds of each subject, where
applicable. For rules about haiku making, please see
Haikus of All Seasons I: The Heavens and The Earth
(2018).

This book is dedicated to the memory of Donald
Keene (June 1922–February 2019), one of the pioneers in
Japanese literature, who introduced and translated many
Japanese classical works, including *Oku no hoso michi*

(*The Narrow Road to Oku*, 1997) by Matsuo Bashō (1644–

November 1694). At Columbia University and elsewhere,

Keen inspired and mentored countless students. In the

wake of the Great East Japan Earthquake of March 2011,

Keene was naturalized in Japan, in order to encourage the

Japanese. He passed away in Tokyo on February 24, 2019.

旅に病で夢は枯野をかけ廻る

(compiled in 笈日記、The Oi Diary, 1695)

Tabi ni yande yume wa kare no o kake meguru

Stricken on a journey,

My dreams go wandering round

Withered fields.

(translation by Donald Keene)

合掌 July 7, 2019

January

Photograph 1. The Super Blue Blood Moon—the

coincidence of the largest moon of the year, the second full

moon within a month, and a complete lunar eclipse,

January 31, 2018, courtesy of © Morrell Chance, 2018.

初日の出

　　東雲を突き

　　　　天を突く

はつひので

　　しののめをつき

　　　　てんをつく

季語　　初日の出（はつひので、新年をさす）

東雲（しののめ）は、夜明け前に茜色にそまる空のこと。

Hatsu hinode

shinonome o tsuki

ten o tsuku

The first sunrise of the year

thrusts into the clouds at dawn

and the heaven

Season word: *hatsu hinode* (the sunrise on New Year's

Day; signifies the new year)

初茜

　　　新たな御代の

　　　　　出づる朝

はつあかね

　　　あらたなみよの

　　　　　いづるあさ

季語　初茜（はつあかね、新年）

2019年は、明仁（平成）天皇が退位し、新しい皇紀が始

まる年である。

5

Hatsu akane

aratana miyo no

izuru asa

The dawn on New Year's Day

the new imperial throne

is emerging in this morning

Season word: *hatsu akane* (the dawn on New Year's Day;

new year)

The succession of the imperial reign took place in 2019.

淑気満つ

　　「令和」の光

　　　　満つる空

しゅくきみつ

　　れいわのひかり

　　　　みつるそら

季語　　淑気（しゅくき、新年）

淑気（しゅくき）は、新年を迎え、天地山河いたる所に瑞祥
の気が満ちていること。2019年5月1日、徳仁皇太子が新
天皇即位し、新しい皇紀は、「令和」と命名された。

7

Shukuki mitsu

"Reiwa" no hikari

mitsuru sora

The auspicious atmosphere fills the air

and the light of the new imperial era Reiwa

fills the sky

Season word: *shuku ki mitsu* (the auspicious atmosphere

fills the air; new year)

The Reiwa imperial era began on May 1, 2019, replacing

the Heisei imperial era.

初富士や

　　有明海の

　　　　月望む

はつふじや

　　ありあけかいの

　　　　つきのぞむ

季語　　初富士（はつふじ、新年）

有明海は、九州最大の湾で、南は八代海とつながってい

る。この月は、夜明けに西空に沈みゆく月をさす。

Hatsu Fuji ya

Ariake kai no

tsuki nozomu

Mt. Fuji at dawn on New Year's Day

looking to the west

wishing to see the moon

setting in the Ariake Sea

Season word: *hatsu Fuji* (the first view of Mt. Fuji on New Year's Day; new year)

The Ariake (*lit.*, dawn) Sea is the largest sea in the Kyūshū region, one of the four major islands of Japan, in the west.

去年今年

　　列島中の

　　　　畏る

こぞことし

　　れっとうじゅうの

　　　　かしこまる

季語　去年今年（こぞことし、新年）

11

Kozo kotoshi

rettō jū no

kashikomaru

Reminiscing about last year on New Year's Day

the whole Japanese archipelago

is solemn

Season word: *kozo kotoshi* (reminiscing about last year on

New Year's Day; new year)

初霞

　　出雲大社の

　　　　息使ひ

はつがすみ

　　いずもたいしゃの

　　　　いきづかい

季語　初霞（はつがすみ、新年）

13

Hatsu gasumi

Izumo taisha no

iki zukai

The morning mist on New Year's Day

is embracing the breath

of Izumo Grand Shrine

Season word: *hatsu kasumi* (the morning mist on New

Year's Day; new year)

Izumo Grand Shrine in Shimane prefecture is believed to

be the oldest Shinto shrine in Japan, even predating Ise

Grand Shrine.

年新た

　　ホルストの観た

　　　　明けの明星

としあらた

　　ホルストのみた

　　　　あけのみょうじょう

季語　　年新た（としあらた、新年）

明けの明星は、金星をさす。グスタフ・ホルスト（1874 年
−1934 年）作曲の『惑星』の第二曲は、「金星、平和をもた
らす者」である。

Toshi arata

Horusuto no mita

Ake no myōjō

The new year

the Morning Star is rising

in the way Holst portrayed

Season word: *toshi arata* (the new year; new year)

The Morning Star refers to Venus, which Gustav Holst
(1874–1934) composed as "Venus: The Bringer of Peace"
in *The Planets*.

初凪や

　　風の隙間を

　　　　撫でにけり

はつなぎや

　　かぜのすきまを

　　　　なでにけり

季語　初凪（はつなぎ、新年）

Hatsu nagi ya

kaze no sukima o

nade ni keri

The morning calm of the sea on New Year's Day

gently strokes

the gaps in the wind

Season word: *hatsu nagi* (the morning calm of the sea on

New Year's Day; new year)

雪の花

　　兎の毛より

　　　生まれたり

ゆきのはな

　　うさぎのけより

　　　うまれたり

季語　　雪の花（ゆきのはな、冬）

雪の花は、雪の結晶のこと。1936年、北海道大学の中谷宇吉

郎（なかやうちきろう、1900年-1962年）研究チームにより、雪

の結晶が初めて人工的に作られた。雪の結晶には核となるもの

が必要で、自然にできるものは、空気中の微粒子（小さなちり）

が核となるが、同研究チームは、羅紗の毛や兎の毛を核とした

雪の結晶を作る実験に成功した。

Yuki no hana

    usagi no ke yori

        umare tari

The snowflake

    was born

        out of the hair of the hare

Season word: *yuki no hana* (*lit.*, "snow flower" refers to snowflakes; winter)

In 1936, Nakaya Ukichirō (1900–1962) succeeded in creating artificial snowflakes for the first time in the world, by using the hair of a hare as a core of the snowflakes.

「赤い月」

　　　凍空駆ける

　　　シャッター音

あかいつき

　　　いてぞらかける

　　　　　シャッターおん

季語　凍空（いてぞら、冬）

2018年1月31日は、皆既月食で、しかも、スーパームーン、且つ、ブルームーン（同じ月の二度目の満月）であった。

"Akai tsuki"

    ite zora kakeru

        shattā on

The Red Moon

    the sounds of camera shutters

        are galloping through the freezing sky

Season word: *ite zora* (freezing sky; winter)

The Super Blue Blood Moon—the coincidence of the

largest moon of the year, the second full moon within a

month, and a complete lunar eclipse—occurred on January

31, 2018, and photographers around the world chased the

moon to catch this rare spectacle in the night sky.

February

Photograph 2. Nachi Great Falls

虎落笛

　　キーン先生

　　　　偲び啼く

もがりぶえ

　　キーンせんせい

　　　　しのびなく

季語　　虎落笛（もがりぶえ、冬）

2019 年 2 月 24 日、日本文学研究第一人者であるドナル

ド・キーン（鬼怒鳴門、1922 年–2019 年）コロンビア大学名

誉教授が死去した。2011 年 3 月の東日本大震災後、日

本人を鼓舞するため、日本に帰化した。

25

Mogari bue

    Kiin sensei

        shinobi naku

The aeolian sound of wintry wind

    going through bamboo fences

        sobs at the death of Prof. Keene

Season word: *mogari bue* (the aeolian sound of wintry wind going through bamboo fences; winter).

Kiin sensei refers to Donald Keene (1922–2019), who was naturalized in Japan, in order to encourage the Japanese in the wake of the Great East Japan Earthquake of March 2011, passed away on February 24.

立春や

　　天の計らひ

　　　のごと来たり

りっしゅんや

　　てんのはからい

　　　のごときたり

季語　立春（りっしゅん、春）

俳句では、2月4日の立春から、春となる。

Risshun ya

    ten no hakarai no

        goto kitari

The arrival of spring

    comes

        as if the heavens had planned it

Season word: *Risshun* (arrival of spring, February 4; spring)

In haiku, Risshun on February 4 marks the beginning of spring.

淡雪や

　　儚き想ひ

　　　　溶かしたり

あわゆきや

　　はかなきおもい

　　　　とかしたり

季語　淡雪（あわゆき、春）

Awa yuki ya

    hakanaki omoi

        tokashi tari

The light snow

    melts away

        the unattainable sentiment

Season word: *awa yuki* (light snow; spring)

那智の滝

　　しぶきの放つ

　　　　春の聲

なちのたき

　　しぶきのはなつ

　　　　はるのこえ

季語　春(はる、春)

和歌山県那智勝浦町にある那智の滝は日本三大名瀑・

日本三大神滝の一つである。

Nachi no taki

shibuki no hanatsu

haru no koe

Nachi Great Falls

the splashing water emits

the voice of spring

Season word: *haru* (spring; spring)

Nachi Great Falls, located in Nachi–Katsuura, Wakayama prefecture, is one of the three greatest and holiest waterfalls in Japan.

薄氷や

　　　朝の光の

　　　　　　そっと踏む

うすらいや

　　　あさのひかりの

　　　　　　そっとふむ

季語　薄氷（うすらひ、春）

Usurai ya

    asa no hikari no

        sotto fumu

The thin ice

    the morning light steps on it

        gently

Season word: *usirahi* (thin ice; spring)

土湿る

　　一雨ごとに

　　　　春来たり

つちしめる

　　ひとさめごとに

　　　　はるきたり

季語　春（はる、春）

Tsuchi shimeru

    hito same goto ni

        haru kitari

The soil is moist

    each rain brings

        the spring closer

Season word: *tsuchi shimeru* (the soil is moist; spring)

魚氷に上る

　　鬼怒川の

　　　　光戯る

うおひにのぼる

　　きぬがわの

　　　　ひかりたわむる

季語　魚氷に上る(うおひにのぼる、春)

Uo hi ni noboru

Kinu gawa no

hikari tawamuru

The fish jumps up on the ice

on the Kinu River

and plays with the light

Season word: *uo hi no noboru* (*lit.*, "the fish jumps up on the ice"; spring)

The Kinu River originates in Nikkō, Tochigi prefecture, and merges with the Tone River, the second longest river in Japan, which runs in the Kantō plain.

「飛梅」や

　　津波の里へ

　　　　一つ飛び

とびうめや

　　つなみのさとへ

　　　　ひとっとび

季語　飛梅（とびうめ、春）

菅原道眞の「飛梅」伝説より連想。

Tobi ume ya

    Tsunami no sato e

        hitto tobi

The Flying Plum Blossoms

    travel to the villages

        that have been destroyed by the Tsunami

Season word: *Tobi ume* (The Flying Plum Blossoms; spring)

This alludes to the legend of *Tobi ume*, in which white plum blossoms missed the demoted scholar/poet Sugawara no Michizane (845–903), so that they flew to Dazaifu where he had been sent.

「パール富士」

　　春の夜明けの

　　　　子守唄

パールふじ

　　はるのよあけの

　　　　こもりうた

季語　春（はる、春）

2019年2月20日6時33分、神奈川県横須賀市で、「パール富士」（満月が富士山頂に沈み、あたかも山頂に真珠がのっているように見える現象）が見られた。この日の満月は、2019年のスーパームーンであった。朝焼けに赤く染まる山頂に満月がぽっかりのった。

41

Pāru fuji

    haru no yoake no

        komori uta

Pearl Fuji

    the spring dawn sings

        a lullaby to the moon

Season word: *haru no yoake* (dawn in spring; spring)

Pearl Fuji refers to a rare phenomenon in which a full moon descends on Mt. Fuji at dawn, making the scene look like a pearl sitting on the summit of Mt. Fuji. That on February 20, 2019 was even more spectacular, because the moon was a Super Moon, the largest full moon of the year.

三保の松原

　　羽衣と

　　　　春の曙

みほのまつばら

　　はごろもと

　　　　はるのあけぼの

季語　春(はる、春)

43

Miho no matsu bara

hagoromo to

haru no akebono

The pine grove of Miho

the feathery robe of the celestial muse

in the dawn in the spring

Season word: *haru no akebono* (dawn in spring; spring)

March

Photograph 3. "Fearfully and Wonderfully Made," after

Psalm 139–14, acrylic painting by © Meg Itoh, 2014.

水緩む

　　光の精の

　　　　目醒めたり

みずぬるむ

　　ひかりのせいの

　　　　めざめたり

季語　水緩む（みずぬるむ、春）

Mizu nurumu

hikari no seino

mezame tari

The water is warm

the spirit of the light

is waking up

Season word: *mizu nurumu* (the water is warm; spring)

もの芽や

　　　厚き衣の

　　　　　綻びる

もののめや

　　　あつきころもの

　　　　　ほころびる

季語　もの芽（もののめ、春）

49

Mono no me ya

atsuki koromo no

hokoro biru

The tree buds

are undressing

from their thick coats

Season word: *mono no me* (tree buds; spring)

春雨や

　　眠る大地を

　　　　起こしゆく

はるさめや

　　ねむるだいちを

　　　　おこしゆく

季語　　春雨（はるさめ、春）

51

Haru same ya

nemureru daichi o

okoshi yuku

The spring rain

is awakening the good earth

one field by field

Season word: *haru same* (spring rain; spring)

二輪草

　　　心の絆

　　　　　結ぶ風

にりんそう

　　　こころのきずな

　　　　　むすぶかぜ

季語　二輪草（にりんそう、春）

一つの茎から二つの花茎が伸びる、ニリンソウの花言葉は、
「友情」、「ずっと離れない」。

Nirin sō

kokoro no kizuna

musubu kaze

The soft windflower

the gentle wind is tying

the bond of the two hearts

Season word: *nirin sō* (*lit.*, "two-flowered plant," soft

windflower, *anemone flaccida*; spring)

This plant grows two flowering stems from one stem;

hence the name. Its flower language is "friendship" and "to

be together forever."

風光る

　　万物の祈り

　　　　運ばんと

かぜひかる

　　ばんぶつのいのり

　　　　はこばんと

季語　風光る（かぜひかる、春）

Kaze hikaru

ban butsu no inori

hakoban to

The wind shines

intent on carrying the prayers

for all things

Season word: *kaze hikaru* (the wind shines; spring)

窓越しの

　　日差し柔らか

　　　　シクラメン

まどごしの

　　ひざしやわらか

　　　　シクラメン

季語　シクラメン（春）

Mado goshi no

hizashi yawaraka

shikuraen

The sunlight through the window

softly shines

on the cyclamen

Season word: *shikuramen* (cyclamen; spring)

雛孵る

　　世の煩ひを

　　　　忘れたり

ひなかえる

　　よのわずらいを

　　わすれたり

季語　雛孵る（ひなかえる、春）

Hina kaeru

    yo no wazurai o

        wasure tari

The chicks hatched

    making one forget

        the troubles of the human world

Season word: *hina kaeru* (chicks hatched; spring)

春雷や

　　ベートーベンの

　　　　怒り聴く

しゅんらいや

　　ベートーベンの

　　　　いかりきく

季語　春雷（しゅんらい、春）

ベートーベンの小曲、ロンド・カプリチオ、作品129番、「失

った一文への怒り」（Rondo Capriccio, Op. 129, "Rage

Over a Lost Penny"）より連想。

Shun rai ya

Bētōben no

ikari kiku

The spring thunder and lightning

listen

to the rage of Beethoven

Season word: *shun rai* (the spring thunder and lightning;

spring)

This alludes to Beethoven's temper in general and

specifically to the piano piece, Rondo Capriccio, Op, 129,

"Rage Over a Lost Penny."

貝寄風や

　　　体寄せ合ふ

　　　　　空と海

かいよせや

　　　からだよせあう

　　　　　そらとうみ

季語　　貝寄風（かいよせ、春）

貝寄風（かいよせ）は、3月下旬に吹く強い季節風のこと。

この名前の由来は、聖徳太子の忌日（陰暦2月22日）に

聖徳太子ゆかりの大阪市の四天王寺で行われる聖霊会

（しょうりょうえ）に、季節風により浜辺に打ち寄せられた貝

殻から造花を作って供えた習慣にちなむ。

Kaiyose ya

karada yose au

sora to umi

The late-March wind

makes the sky and the sea

come closer

Season word: *kaiyose* (*lit.*, "seashell gathering wind" refers
to the late-March wind; spring)

This strong seasonal wind is named after the memorial service
for Prince Shōtoku (574–622), conducted in Shiten'nō Temple in
Osaka, on his death anniversary day, February 22 in the
traditional calendar (corresponding the late March today), in
which people made offerings of artificial flowers, made of
seashells, which were blown by the strong seasonal wind.

蜃気楼

　　　　平安絵巻

　　　　　　紐解きぬ

しんきろう

　　　へいあんえまき

　　　　　ひもときぬ

季語　蜃気楼（しんきろう、春）

Shinkirō

Heian emaki

himo toki nu

The spring haze

unrolls

the picture scrolls of the Heian era

Season word: *shinkirō* (mirage; spring)

April

Photograph 4. Dandelion puffs.

春風や

　　　綿毛追ひかけ

　　　　　光笑む

はるかぜや

　　　わたげおいかけ

　　　　　ひかりえむ

季語　春風（はるかぜ、春）

Haru kaze ya

    watage oikake

        hikari emu

The spring wind

    is chasing after the dandelion puffs

        and the light smiles

Season word: *haru kaze* (the spring wind; spring)

紋白蝶

　　薄い緑の

　　　　ヴェール剥ぐ

もんしろちょう

　　うすいみどりの

　　　　ヴェールはぐ

季語　紋白蝶（もんしろちょう、春）

モンシロチョウのサナギは薄緑色。

Mon shiro chō

usui midori no

veiru hagu

The small white butterfly

sheds

its pale green veil

Season word: *mon shiro chō* (the small white butterfly;

spring)

This alludes to the metamorphosis of a butterfly.

朧月

　　独り夜更けに

　　　　花見せり

おぼろづき

　　ひとりよふけに

　　　　はなみせり

季語　朧月（おぼろづき、春）　花見（はなみ、春）

詩歌では、花は通常、桜のことを指す。

Oboro zuki

    hitori yofuke ni

        hanami seri

The hazy spring moon

    is viewing the cherry blossoms

        late at night alone

Season words: *oboro zuki* (hazy spring moon; spring) and

hanami (cherry blossom viewing; spring)

春驟雨

　　キーン先生

　　　　送る朝

はるしゅうう

　　キーンせんせい

　　　　おくるあさ

季語　　春驟雨（はるしゅうう、春のにわか雨、春）

ドナルド・キーン先生のお別れ会が、2019 年 4 月

10 日に東京で行われた。

Haru shūu

    Kiin sensei

        okuru asa

The spring rain shower

    people mourn the death of Prof. Keene

        in the morning

Season word: *haru shūu* (spring rain shower; spring)

On April 10, 2019, a memorial service for Donald Keene (1922–2019) was held in Tokyo, who passed away in February 2019.

淡墨桜

　　　ひとひらと散る

　　　　　その淡さ

うすずみざくら

　　　ひとひらとちる

　　　　　そのうすさ

季語　淡墨桜（うすずみざくら、春）

Usuzumi zakura

hito hira to chiru

sono ususa

The pale white cherry blossoms

are falling petal by petal

as pale as could be

Season word: *Usuzumi zakura* (the pale white cherry

blossoms; spring)

This famous 1,500-year old cherry tree stands in Neodani,

Motosu, Gifu prefecture.

春夕焼

　　宵の明星

　　　　待ち侘びる

はるゆやけ

　　よいのみょうじょう

　　　　まちわびる

季語　春夕焼（はるゆやけ、春）

Haru yuyake

    yoi no myojō

        machi wabiru

The spring sunset glory

    impatiently waits

        for the Evening Star to appear

Season word: *haru yuyake* (spring sunset glory; spring)

真珠星

　　潤む瞳の

　　　　奥の星

しんじゅぼし

　　うるむひとみの

　　　　おくのほし

季語　真珠星（しんじゅぼし、スピカ、春）

スピカは、乙女座のアルファ恒星である。

Shinju boshi

urumu hitomi no

oku no hoshi

The Pearl Star

sees the star

in the tearful eye of the maiden

Season word: *Shinju boshi* (The Pearl Star, Spica; spring)

Spica is the alpha star in the constellation Virgo.

春雨や

　　ヴェローナの愛

　　　　慈しむ

はるさめや

　　ヴェローナのあい

　　　　いつくしむ

季語　春雨（はるさめ、春）

シェークスピアの戯曲「ロミオとジュリエット」およびそれを
題材とした芸術作品（チャイコフスキーの幻想序曲など）へ
のオマージュ。

Haru same ya

Verona no ai

itsuku shimu

The spring rain

tenderly embraces

the love in Verona

Season word: *haru same* (spring rain; spring)

This is a homage to the play *Romeo and Juliet* by William

Shakespeare (1564–1616) and other forms of art that were

inspired by the story, including the *Overture–Fantasy*

Romeo and Juliet by P.I. Tchaikovsky (1840–1893).

登呂遺跡

　　「弥生」の記憶

　　　　掘り起こす

とろいせき

　　やよいのきおく

　　　　ほりおこす

季語　　弥生（やよい、陰暦3月、新暦の4月、春）

静岡県の登呂遺跡（弥生時代の遺跡）の発掘調査は
1974 年春に始まった。

Toro iseki

Yayoi no kioku

hori okosu

The Ruins of Toro

the memories of Yayoi

have been restored

Season word: *Yayoi* (March in the traditional calendar that

corresponds to April today, and also refers to the ancient

period, arguably from 400 BC to 300 AD; spring)

Excavations of the Ruins of Toro in Shizuoka, Shizuoka

prefecture, began in the spring of 1947, which marked the

first archaeological excavation in Japan.

春夕立

　　小枝の雨露の

　　　　数珠つなぎ

はるゆだち

　　こえだのうろの

　　　　じゅずつなぎ

季語　春夕立（はるゆだち、春）

Haru yudachi

koeda no uro no

juzu tsunagi

The spring rain shower

the dewdrops on the little branch

look like Buddhist rosary beads

Season word: *haru yudachi* (spring rain shower; spring)

Juzu, formally made of 108 beads, refers to a rosary used in

Buddhist prayers.

May

Photograph 5. Celestial muse (*Hiten*) at Hōkai Temple,

Kyoto, under Wikimedia Commons license, "Hiten,"

March 14, 2006, https://ja.wikipedia.org/wiki/飛天

#/media/ファイル: Tennin_(Japanese_angel).jpg.

草萌ゆる

　　遥かな大地

　　　　ブラジルへ

くさもゆる

　　はるかなだいち

　　　　ブラジルへ

季語　　草萌ゆる（くさもゆる、春）

石川達三は、『蒼氓』（1935 年）で、邦人のブラジル移民の
悲愴な有様を描いた。

Kusa moyuru

haruka na daichi

Burajiru e

The grass spouts are budding

in the faraway land

of Brazil

Season word: *haru yudachi* (spring rain shower; spring)

In Sōbō (*lit.*, people at large or immigrants, 1935/1939), Ishikawa Tatsuzō (1905–1985) poignantly depicted the plight of Japanese immigrants to Brazil.

山笑ふ

　　　風に色つけ

　　　　　飛ばしたり

やまわらう

　　　かぜにいろつけ

　　　　　とばしたり

季語　山笑ふ（やまわらう、春）

Yama warau

kaze ni iro tsuke

tobashi tari

The mountain smiles

it paints the wind with the color of the spring

and blows it out

Season word: *yama warau* (the mountain smiles; spring)

花一華

　　　切なき想ひ

　　　　　揺れる風

はないちげ

　　　せつなきおもい

　　　　　ゆれるかぜ

季語　花一華（はないちげ、アネモネの雅語、春）

アネモネは、ラテン語の「風」に由来し、その花言葉は、

「儚い恋」、「恋の苦しみ」である。

Hana ichige

    setsunaki omoi

        yureru kaze

The anemone

    knows the unattainable love

        and the wind swings

Season word: *hana ichige* (anemone, windflower; spring)

Deriving from the Greek myth of Aphrodite and Adonis, in which the blood of Adonis became the anemone, the flower language of the anemone is "forsaken love" and "agony of love."

奈良の春

　　薬師寺の飛天

　　　　生き還る

ならのはる

　　やくしじのひてん

　　　　いきかえる

季語　　春（はる、春）

細川護熙元首相（もりひろ）は、奈良の薬師寺慈恩殿修復
の一貫として、天女の画を描き、2019年、全108枚（66面）
の障壁画を奉納した。

Nara no haru

Yakushi ji no hiten

iki kaeru

The spring in Nara

the celestial muses of Yakushi Temple

were revived

Season word: *haru* (spring; spring)

In 2019, a total of 108 newly created wall paintings (on 66

façades) were completed and donated to the Jion Hall of

Yakushi Temple in Nara. They were painted by former

prime minister Hosokawa Morihiro, a descendent of the

aristocratic rulers of the Fujiwara clan.

麗らかに

　　小鳩微睡む

　　　　仏の掌

うららかに

　　こばとまどろむ

　　　　ほとけのて

季語　麗らか（うららか、春）

Uraraka ni

kobato madoromu

hotoke no te

The fine springtime

the dove is dozing

on the palm of the statue of Buddha

Season word: *uraraka* (a fine springtime; spring)

春の風や

　　欄間の雉子の

　　　　つがい啼く

はるのかぜ

　　らんまのきじの

　　　　つがいなく

季語　春風（はるのかぜ、春）

Haru no kaze

　　ran'ma no kiji no

　　　　tsugai naku

The spring wind

　　makes the woodcarving

　　　　of the Japanese green pheasant

　　　　　　couple cry

Season word: *haru no kaze* (spring wind; spring)

夫婦星

　　　永遠に寄り添ふ

　　　　契りなり

めおとぼし

　　　とわによりそう

　　　　ちぎりなり

季語　夫婦星（めおとぼし、春）

おとめ座のスピカとうしかい座のアルクトゥルスは、（春の）

夫婦星と呼ばれる。

Meoto boshi

   towa ni yori sou

      chigiri nari

The Couple Stars

   are destined to shine

      side by side forever

Season word: *Meoto boshi* ("The Couple Stars" refer to

Arcturus and Spica; spring)

Arcturus in the constellation Bootes and Spica in the

constellation Virgo are called the Couple Stars of Spring.

「地質の日」

　　アンモナイトの

　　　　夢開く

ちしつのひ

　　アンモナイトの

　　　　ゆめひらく

季語　「地質の日」（ちしつのひ、夏）

5月10日は、「地質の日」。

俳句では、5月5日の立夏から、夏となる。

Chishitsu no hi

anmonaito no

yume hiraku

The Day of Geology

the dreams of ammonite

unfold

Season word: *Chishitsu no hi* (Day of Geology in Japan,

May 10; summer)

In haiku, May 5 marks the beginning of summer.

長良川

　　　光るせせらぎ

　　　　鮎の風

ながらがわ

　　　ひかるせせらぎ

　　　　あゆのかぜ

季語　鮎（あゆ、夏）

水源を岐阜県に持つ長良川は、日本三大清流の一つ。

鮎釣りで有名。

Nagara gawa

hikaru seseragi

ayu no kaze

The Nagara River

the stream is shining

and sends forth the fragrance of sweetfish

Season word: *ayu* (sweetfish; summer)

The Nagara River, originating in Gifu prefecture, is one of

the three cleanest rivers in Japan. The sweetfish has a

sweet scent.

青葉雨

　　故国の命

　　　　蘇る

あおばあめ

　　ここくのいのち

　　　　よみがえる

季語　青葉雨（あおばあめ、夏）

ブラジル移民の壮絶な歴史。

Aoba ame

kokoku no inochi

yomi gaeru

The refreshing rain on the green leaves

the life of the homeland

has come back

Season word: *kaze hikaru* (the refreshing rain on the green

leaves; spring)

The Japanese immigrants to Brazil toiled and cultivated the

barren land of Brazil.

June

Photograph 6. Rainbow, June 2019.

走り梅雨

　　一色足りぬ

　　　　虹の橋

はしりづゆ

　　ひといろたりぬ

　　　　にじのはし

季語　走り梅雨（はしりづゆ、夏）　虹（にじ、夏）

走り梅雨（はしりづゆ）は、梅雨の季節に入る前ぶれの雨
のこと。

Hashiri zuyu

    hito iro tarinu

        niji no hashi

The early rainy season

    the rainbow bridge

        lacks one color

Season words: *hashiri zuyu* (the early rainy season; summer) and *niji* (rainbow; summer)

黒南風や

　　　緑騒めく

　　　　　山と空

くろはえや

　　　みどりざわめく

　　　　　やまとそら

季語　黒南風（くろはえ、夏）

黒南風（くろはえ）は、梅雨入りの暗い空に吹く湿った南風のこと。

Kurohae ya

    midori zawameku

      yama to sora

The dark, wet wind

    the green leaves are agitated

      in the sky and the mountain

Season word: *kurohae* (the dark, wet wind at the beginning

of the rainy season; summer)

梅雨の闇

　　汽笛を包む

　　　靄の聲

つゆのやみ

　　きてきをつつむ

　　　もやのこえ

季語　梅雨の闇（つゆのやみ、夏）

梅雨の闇は、梅雨の時期、厚い雲に覆われた日の様子を
さす。

Tsuyu no yami

    kiteki o tsutsumu

       moya no koe

The darkness in the rainy season

    the voice of dense mist engulfs

       the sound of the train whistle

Season word: *tsuyu no yami* (dark atmosphere in the rainy season; summer)

蛍火や

　　雨粒の音と

　　　　シンコペーション

ほたるびや

　　あまつぶのねと

　　　　シンコペーション

季語　　蛍火（ほたるび、夏）

Hotarubi ya

    ama tsubu no ne to

        shinkopēhon

The fireflies

    are syncopating

        with the raindrops

Season word: *hotaru bi* (firefly flickering; summer)

梅雨の星

　　　暗雲の

　　　　　天を導く

つゆのほし

　　　あんうんの

　　　　　てんをみちびく

季語　梅雨の星（つゆのほし、アルクトゥルス、夏）

春から夏にかけて、オレンジ色に輝く、うしかい座のアルク

トゥルスは、最も明るい星の一つ。

Tsuyu no hoshi

an'un no ten o

michibiku

The star in the rainy season

guides the heavens

among the dark clouds

Season word: *tsuyu no hoshi* (the star in the rainy season; summer)

The star in the rainy season specifically refers to Arcturus in the constellation Bootes, which is one of the brightest stars in the night sky.

夏の宵

　　　弓月の明かり

　　　　　充つるなり

なつのよい

　　　ゆづきのあかり

　　　　　みつるなり

季語　夏の宵（なつのよい、夏）

弓月（ゆづき）は、半月の文語的表現。夏の宵は、半月で
も充分明るく感ずる。

Natsu no yoi

    yuzuki no akari

        mitsuru nari

The summer night

    the waxing half moon is bright enough

        to light the sky

Season word: *natsu no yoi* (the summer night; summer)

Yuzuki *(lit.*, "bow-like moon") refers to the waxing half moon or the first quarter moon.

仁淀川

　　ミント・ブルーと

　　　　白き滝

によどがわ

　　ミント・ブルーと

　　　　しろきたき

季語　　滝（たき、夏）

仁淀川（によどがわ）は、愛媛県から高知県を経由して太平洋へと注ぐ一級河川。その美しい清流は、「仁淀ブルー」と呼ばれる。

Niyodo gawa

minto burū to

shiroki taki

The Niyodo River

is adorned by mint-blue water

and white waterfalls

Season word: *taki* (waterfalls; summer)

The Niyodo River, running from Ehime prefecture to Kochi

prefecture, and then into the Pacific Ocean, is known for its

clean, beautiful water, referred to as the "Niyodo blue."

万緑や

　　　サングラス染め

　　　　　いよ深し

ばんりょくや

　　　サングラスそめ

　　　　　いよふかし

季語　万緑（ばんりょく、夏）

Banryoku ya

    san gurasu some

        iyo fukashi

The green leaves all over

    color the sunglasses

        and look even greener

Season word: *ban ryoku* (green leaves all over; summer)

夫婦岩

　　ダイアモンド富士

　　　拝む夏至

めおといわ

　　ダイアモンドふじ

　　　おがむげし

季語　夏至（げし、夏）

三重県伊勢市の二見ヶ浦では、夏至の頃、夫婦岩の間から、約200キロ離れたダイアモンド富士（日の出の位置と富士山が重な理、富士山頂からダイアモンドが輝いているように見える現象）が見える。この現象は、夏至の前後と6月30日頃の一年に二度のみ見られる。

Meoto iwa

Daiamondo Fuji

ogamu geshi

At the Couple Rocks

the Summer Solstice greets

the Diamond Fuji

Season word: *geshi* (summer solstice; summer)

The Diamond Fuji refers to a phenomenon in which the sun rises

from the top of Mt. Fuji, making it look like a diamond shining

on the summit of Mt. Fuji. The Diamond Fuji can be seen in

between the two sacred rocks, the Couple Rocks in Ise, Mie

prefecture—124 miles away from Mt. Fuji—only twice a year;

around the summer solstice and on June 30.

夏の夕

　　　月と金星

　　　　　すれ違ふ

なつのゆう

　　　つきときんせい

　　　　　すれちがう

季語　夏の夕（なつのゆう、夏）

夏の夕方、新月と金星は、夕暮れ時がまだ明るいために、

西空に沈む前に一緒に見える時間が少ない。

Natsu no yū

    tsuki to kinsei

        sure chigau

The summer evening

    Moon and Venus

        missed each other

Season word: *natsu no yū* (the summer evening; summer)

July

Photograph 7. "Double sun" at sunset, July 2019.

梓川

　　河童橋にて

　　　　涼む風

あずさがわ

　　かっぱばしにて

　　　　すずむかぜ

季語　涼む(すずむ、夏)

河童橋は、長野県松本市、乗鞍高原・上高地の梓川にか

かる吊り橋。北アルプスの焼岳や穂高連峰が見える。

Azusa gawa

Kappa bashi nite

suzumu kaze

The Azusa River

the wind is cooling off

at the Kappa Bridge

Season word: *suzumu* (to cool off; summer)

The Azusa River runs in the Norikura volcanic mountain

range of the Northern Japan Alps in Nagano prefecture.

The Kappa Bridge is located in Kami kōchi in Norikura.

山滴る

　　大正池の

　　　　朝の靄

やましたたる

　　たいしょういけの

　　　　あさのもや

季語　　山滴る（やましたたる、夏）

大正池は、1915 年（大正 4 年）6 月 6 日に、梓川が焼岳

（乗鞍火山帯の唯一の活火山）の噴火で堰き止められて

できた池。白樺の立ち枯れ（たちかれ）が美しく、国の特別

名勝・特別天然記念物に指定される。

Yama shitataru

Taishō ike no

asa no moya

The mountain with the rush of green

Lake Taishō is surrounded

by the morning mist

Season word: *yama shitataru* (a mountain in the summer

fresh with the rush of green; summer)

The scenic Lake Taishō in Matsumoto, Nagano prefecture,

was created when the volcanic eruption of Mt. Yake

blocked the flow of the Azusa River.

大夕焼

　　二重の太陽

　　　　現るる

おおゆやけ

　　ふたえのたいよう

　　　　あらわるる

季語　　夕焼（ゆやけ、ゆうやけ、夏）

二重の太陽は、日没時に、太陽が水平線や地平線の近く
で変形して見える現象（「変形太陽」）の一種。暖気と冷気
が接触して、光が屈折することにより発生する蜃気楼。

Ō yukake

    futae no taiyō

        arawa ruru

The glorious sunset

    the double sun

        has appeared

Season word: *yukake* (sunset glory; summer)

This refers to a phenomenon in which a sun looks deformed at the horizon at sunset, due to optical refraction.

真夏の夜

　　喝采響く

　　　　パックの森

まなつのよ

　　かっさいひびく

　　　　パックのもり

季語　真夏の夜（まなつのよ、夏）

シェークスピアの『真夏の夜の夢』およびこの戯曲を題材
とした、他の芸術作品（メンデルスゾーンの『真夏の夜の
夢・序曲』、同・劇付随音楽』など）へのオマージュ。

Ma natsu no yo

kassai hibiku

Pakku no mori

The midsummer night

the applause reverberates

in the forest of Puck

Season word: *ma matsu no yo* (midsummer night; summer)

This is a homage to A Midsummer Night's Dream by

William Shakespeare (1564–1616) and various performing

arts inspired by the play, including the overture and

incidental music by Felix Mendelssohn (1809–1847).

北欧の

　　　白夜に眠る

　　　　　星のあり

ほくおうの

　　　はくやにねむる

　　　　　ほしのあり

季語　白夜（はくや、夏）

Hokuō no

    haku ya ni nemuru

        hoshi no ari

The stars sleep

    in the white night

        in Northern Europe

Season word: *haku ya* (the white night; summer)

夏の天

　　「月の雫」を

　　　　抱きたり

なつのてん

　　つきのしずくを

　　　　いだきたり

季語　　夏（なつ、夏）

「月の雫」は、真真珠の別名。

Natsu no ten

    tsuki no shizoku o

        idaki tari

The summer sky

    embraces

        the moon drops

Season word: *natsu no ten* (summer sky; summer)

The "moon drops" refer to pearls.

御来迎

　　　立山の峰

　　　　　跪く

ごらいごう

　　　たてやまのみね

　　　　　ひざまづく

季語　御来迎（ごらいごう、夏）

御来迎（ごらいごう）は、山頂で見る日の出のこと。立山は
富山県東部にある霊山で、登山信仰が盛んであった。

Go raigō

Tateyama no mine

hizama zuku

The sunrise at the summit of Mt. Tate

all the surrounding ridges kneel down

and make prayers

Season word: *Go raigō* (sunrise at the summit of a

mountain; summer)

Mt. Tate is one of the mountains that constitute the

Northern Japan Alps.

北穂高

　　　雪渓を踏む

　　　　　這松と靴

きたほたか

　　　せっけいをふむ

　　　　　はいまつとくつ

季語　　雪渓（せっけい、夏）

Kita Hotaka

    sekkei o fumu

        haimatsu to kutsu

Mt. Northern Hotaka

    the crawling pines and shoes

        are stepping on the valley of frozen snow

Season word: *sekkei* (valley of frozen snow in the summer; summer)

Mt. Northern Hotaka is part of the Northern Japan Alps.

夏の月

　　　タクラマカンの

　　　　　絹の道

なつのつき

　　　タクラマカンの

　　　　　きぬのみち

季語　　夏の月（なつのつき、夏）

タクラマカン砂漠は、中央アジア、タリム盆地にある砂漠。

Natsu no tsuki

Taklamakan no

Shiruku rōdo

The summer moon

lights the Silk Road

in the Taklamakan Desert

Season word: *natsu no tsuki* (the summer moon; summer)

蠍座や

　　　木星に

　　　　　追われるが如座す

さそりざや

　　　もくせいに

　　　　　おわれるがごとざす

季語　　蠍座（さそりざ、夏）

夏の夜空に木星が君臨し、居場所を失ったような蠍座。

153

Sasori za ya

Mokusei ni owareru

ga goto zasu

The constellation Scorpius

stands as if

it were being chased by Jupiter

Season word: *Sasori za* (the constellation Scorpius;

summer)

August

Photograph 8. Sunset glory, August 2018.

炎帝や

　　見えない星を

　　　　焦がしたり

えんていや

　　みえないほしを

　　　　こがしたり

季語　炎帝（えんてい、夏を司る神、太陽、夏）

Entei ya

    mienai hoshi o

        kogashi tari

The mighty summer sun

    burns

        the invisible stars in the daylight

Season word: *entei* (burning summer sun; summer)

雲の峰

　　　嘶の行く

　　　　　糸杉の道

くものみね

　　　いななきのいく

　　　　　いとすぎのみち

季語　雲の峰（くものみね、入道雲、夏）

159

Kumo no mine

    inanaki no iku

        itosugi no michi

The towering clouds

    the horse's neighing is trotting

        on the road of cypresses

Season word: *kumo no mine* (towering clouds,

cumulonimbus clouds; summer)

日盛りや

　　天の岩戸の

　　　　皆既食

ひざかりや

　　あまのいわとの

　　　　かいきしょく

季語　　日盛り（ひざかり、夏）

天照大神がお隠れになった「天の岩戸」の神話は、皆既

日食を暗示するというのが通説である。

Hi zakari ya

Ama no iwato no

kaiki nisshoku

At the hottest time of the day

the total solar eclipse

covered the Rock Cave of the Sun Goddess

Season word: *hi zakari* (the hottest time of the day in the summer; summer)

The legend of the Rock Cave of the Sun Goddess in Japanese mythology is generally considered to suggest a total solar eclipse.

夕焼け空

　　想ひのままに

　　　　走る刷毛

ゆやけぞら

　　おもいのままに

　　はしるはけ

季語　夕焼け空（ゆやけぞら、夏）

雄大な夕焼け空は、大胆に彩られたターナーの絵画を彷

彿させる。

Yuyake zora

omoi no mama ni

hashiru hake

The sunset glory sky

the blush in the air paints the sky

as it pleases

Season word: *yuyake zora* (sky with sunset glory; summer)

涼風や

　　　津波の里を

　　　　　　吹き抜ける

すずかぜや

　　　つなみのさとを

　　　　　　ふきぬける

季語　　涼風（すずかぜ、夏）

Suzu kaze ya

Tsunami no sato o

fuki nukeru

The cool breeze in the summer

blows through the village

that was destroyed by the Tsunami

Season word: *suzu kaze* (cool breeze in the summer;

summer)

The Tsunami refers to that caused by the Great East Japan

Earthquake of March 2011.

阿智の夏

　　満天の星

　　　　游びたり

あちのなつ

　　まんてんのほし

　　　　あそびたり

季語　夏(なつ、夏)

長野県阿智村は、アマチュア天体観測で村興しに励んで
いる。

Achi no natsu

    manten no hoshi

      asobi tari

In Achi village

    millions of stars in the heavens

      are having fun

Season word: *natsu* (summer; summer)

Achi village, Nagano prefecture, is promoting tourism for
night sky watching during the summer.

北斗星

　　　夏空巡り

　　　　　仔を護る

ほくとせい

　　　なつぞらめぐり

　　　　　こをまもる

季語　夏空（なつぞら、夏）

北斗星（北斗七星、おおぐま座）は、毎日、こぐま座（北極星）の周りを回る。

Hokuto sei

natsu zora meguri

ko o mamoru

The Big Dipper

circles in the summer sky

guarding the Little Bear

Season word: *natsu zora* (summer sky; summer)

The Big Dipper consists of seven bright stars of the
constellation Ursa Major (the Big Bear), whereas the Little
Dipper stands for the constellation Ursa Minor (the Little
Bear) whose alpha star is Polaris, the North Star.

ドドーン！

　　スターマインを

　　　　月と観る

ドドーン！

　　スターマインを

　　　　つきとみる

季語　スターマイン（大規模な連続仕掛け花火、夏）

花火大会の花形、スターマインは月まで届くような圧巻。

Do dōn!

Sutā main o

tsuki to miru

Boom, boom!

One watches the fireworks show of star mines

along with the moon

Season word: *Sutā main* (star mine fireworks that make a

rapid-fire series of bursts; summer)

彦星と

　　織姫の宵

　　　　伝へのごとく

ひこぼしと

　　おりひめのよい

　　　　つたえのごとく

季語　彦星（ひこぼし、秋）　織姫（おりひめ、秋）

彦星と織姫の七夕伝説（旧暦の7月7日は、現在の8月7日頃）。

俳句では、8月7日（立秋）から秋となる。

Hiko boshi to

Ori hime no yoi

tsutae no gotoku

Altair and Vega

meet tonight

as has been told in the legend

Season words: *Hiko boshi* (Altair; autumn) and *Ori hime* (Vega; autumn)

Legend has it that Altair and Vega meet only once a year on July 7 in the traditional calendar, which roughly corresponds to August 7 today. In haiku, August 7 marks the beginning of autumn.

天の川

　　　無数の瞳

　　　　　星と寝る

あまのがわ

　　　むすうのひとみ

　　　　　ほしとねる

季語　天の川（あまのがわ、秋）

Ama no gawa

    musū no hitomi

        hoshi to neru

The Milky Way

    countless eyes

        are sleeping with the stars

Season word: *Ama no gawa* (the Milky Way; autumn)

September

Photograph 9. The score of Piano Sonata No. 14 in C#
minor, commonly known as the "Moonlight Sonata," by
Ludwig van Beethoven.

初嵐

　　　はっと戸惑ふ

　　　　　翅の音

はつあらし

　　　はっととまどう

　　　　　はねのおと

季語　初嵐（はつあらし、秋）

179

Hatsu arashi

hatto tomadou

hane no oto

The first strong wind in autumn

makes the wings of the insect

suddenly bewildered

Season word: *hatsu arashi* (the first strong wind in

autumn; autumn)

秋麗

　　　金の穂波の

　　　　　　運ぶ風

あきうらら

　　　きんのほなみの

　　　　　　はこぶかぜ

季語　秋麗（あきうらら、秋）

Aki urara

kin no honami no

hakobu kaze

The beautiful fine day in autumn

the golden waves of the grass blades

carry the wind

Season word: *aki urara* (beautiful fine day in autumn;

autumn)

流れ星

　　月の女神の

　　　　使者となり

ながれぼし

　　つきのめがみの

　　　　ししゃとなり

季語　流れ星（ながれぼし、秋）

Nagare boshi

tsuki no megami no

shisha to nari

The shooting star

became the messenger of

the moon goddess

Season word: *nagare boshi* (shooting star; autumn)

待宵月

　　　膨らむ心

　　　　　明日の月

まちよいづき

　　　ふくらむこころ

　　　　　あすのつき

季語　　待宵月（まちよいづき、満月の1日前の月、秋）

Machiyoi zuki

fukuramu kokoro

asu no tsuki

The fourteenth-night moon

fills one's heart

as it waxes into the full moon tomorrow

Season word: *machiyoi zuki* (*lit.*, the moon one day before

the full moon, the fourteenth-night moon; autumn)

かぐや姫

　　　月夜の涙

　　　　　海となり

かぐやひめ

　　　つきよのなみだ

　　　　　うみとなり

季語　月夜(つきよ、満月の夜、秋)

Kaguya hime

    tsuki yo no namida

      umi to nari

Princess Kaguya

    her tears on the full moon night

      have become the ocean

Season word: *tsuki yo* (full moon night; autumn)

This refers to a folktale about Princess Kaguya who was

sent from the moon.

月今宵

　　明日には欠ける

　　　　定めかな

つきこよい

　　あすにはかける

　　　　さだめかな

季語　月今宵（つきこよい、中秋の名月、秋）

Tsuki koyoi

asu niwa kakeru

sadame kana

The full moon tonight

its fate is

to wane tomorrow

Season word: *tsuki koyoi* (*lit.*, "tonight's moon" refers to

the mid-autumn full moon, Harvest Moon; autumn)

下弦月

　　ベートベンの

　　　　聴くソナタ

かげんづき

　　ベートベンの

　　　　きくソナタ

季語　下弦月（かげんづき、秋）

ソナタは、ベートベンの「月光ソナタ」第14番、嬰ハ短調を
さす。

Kagen zuki

Bētōsben no

kiku sonata

The last quarter moon

Beethoven listens

to the sonata

Season word: *kagen zuki* (*lit.*, "waning bow-like moon"

refers to the last quarter moon; autumn)

The sonata refers to Piano Sonata No. 14 in C# minor

"Quasi una fantasia," Op. 27, No 2, commonly known as

the "Moonlight Sonata," by Ludwig van Beethoven (1770–

1827).

観月や

　　七十九回

　　　　木星は？

かんげつや

　　しちじゅうきゅうかい

　　　　もくせいは？

季語　観月（かんげつ、月見、秋）

2018 年 7 月米国研究チームの発表によると、木星の衛星

（月）を新たに 12 個発見し、合計数が 79 個に増えた。

Kangetsu ya

shichijū kyū kai

Mokusei wa?

The moon viewing

are there seventy-nine times

for Jupiter?

Season word: *kangetsu* (moon viewing; autumn)

In July 2018, a US. Research team discovered 12 additional moons of Jupiter, making a total of 79 moons for the planet.

星月夜

　　守護神飛びし

　　　　朱雀門

ほしづきよ

　　しゅごしんとびし

　　　　すざくもん

季語　星月夜（ほしづきよ、秋）

朱雀（中国の伝説上の神聖な鳥）は南の守護神で、朱雀
門は、平城京や平安京の南に面する正門であった。

Hoshi zuki yo

   shugoshin tobishi

      Suzaku mon

The bright starry night

   the sacred red bird used to guard

      the Gate of Suzaku

Season word: *hoshi zuki yo* (a bright starry night without the moon; autumn)

Suzaku ("sacred red bird") was the guardian of the Gate of Suzaku, the southern main gate of the Imperial Palace in the ancient period.

秋夕焼

　　月と金星

　　　　巡り合ひ

あきゆやけ

　　つきときんせい

　　　　めぐりあい

季語　秋夕焼（あきゆやけ、秋）

夏の宵にはよく見えなかった三日月と金星が、秋には、西
空に同時に見えるようになる。

Aki yuyake

tsuki to kinsei

meguri au

The autumn sunset glory

the Moon and Venus

had a brief encounter

Season word: *aki yuyake* (sunset glory in autumn; autumn)

In autumn, the crescent moon and Venus can be seen

setting together in the western sky; this was difficult to see

during the summer.

October

Photograph 10. Lake Taishō, Kami-kōchi, Matsumoto,

Nagano prefecture, under Wikimedia Commons license,

"At Taisho-ike," September 20, 2009,

https://commons.wikimedia.org/wiki/File:Kamikochi_Tais

ho-ike04n3200.jpg.

秋の聲

　　音信川の

　　　　足湯かな

あきのこえ

　　おとずれがわの

　　　　あしゆかな

季語　秋の聲（あきのこえ、秋）

山口県長門市の湯本温泉を流れる音信川（おとずれがわ）
は、「おとずれ足湯」で有名。

Aki no koe

    Otozure gawa no

        ashi yu kana

The voice of autumn

    is gently blowing toward the footbath

        by the Otozure River

Season word: *aki no koe* (the voice of autumn; autumn)

The Nagato–Yumoto hot spring resort in Nagato,

Yamaguchi prefecture, is famous for outdoor footbaths

installed along the Otozure River.

朝霧や

　　立ち枯れ消えし

　　　　大正池

あさぎりや

　　たちかれきえし

　　　　たいしょういけ

季語　　朝霧（あさぎり、秋）

1915 年（大正 46 年）6 月、梓川が焼岳の噴火で堰き止め
られてできた大正池は、白樺の立ち枯れが美しく、国の特
別名勝・特別天然記念物に指定されたが、年々土砂流が
流れこみ、現在は、昔の姿をとどめていない。

Asa giri ya

    tachi kare kieshi

        Taishō ike

The morning mist

    the standing dead birches at Lake Taishō

        have disappeared

Season word: *aki no giri* (morning mist; autumn)

Taishō Lake in Kami kōchi, Nagano prefecture, is famous for a mystical scene of standing dead birches surrounded by dense fog; however, in recent years the lake has shrunk due to the accumulation of debris flow.

紅葉狩り

　　　拾ふその手と

　　　　　頬の色

もみじがり

　　　ひろうそのてと

　　　　　ほほのいろ

季語　　紅葉狩り（もみじがり、秋）

Momiji gari

hirou sono te to

hoho no iro

The fall foliage viewing

the hand that is picking up the maple leaves

and the cheeks turn colors

Season word: *momiji gari* (maple fall foliage viewing;

autumn)

栗名月

　　　恵那の蒸篭の

　　　　　湯気の立つ

くりめいげつ

　　　えなのせいろの

　　　　　ゆげのたつ

季語　栗名月（くりめいげつ、秋）

栗名月は、陰暦9月13日の月（新暦10月中旬頃）のこと。

岐阜恵那地方の中津川は、栗きんとんで有名。

Kuri meigetsu

Ena no seiro no

yuge no tatsu

The Chestnut Moon

the steam of cooking chestnut

ascends to the moon

Season word: *Kuri meigetsu* ("Chestnut Moon"; autumn).

This moon refers to the thirteenth-night moon in September

in the traditional calendar, which falls in mid-October

today. This moon resembles a chestnut and people offered

chestnuts, a seasonal produce, to the moon; hence the name.

Nakatsugawa in the Ena region, in Gifu prefecture, is

famous for sweets made of cooked chestnuts.

星降る夜

　　　パンドラの箱

　　　　　開けたり

ほしふるよ

　　　パンドラのはこ

　　　　　ひらけたり

季語　　星降る夜（ほしふるよ、秋）

「パンドラの箱」は、ギリシア神話の一説。

Hoshi furu yo

    Pandora no hako

        hirake tari

The night sky filled with stars

    as if the Pandora's Box

        had opened

Season word: *hoshi furu yo* (the night sky filled with stars; autumn)

寝待ち月

　　源氏の君は

　　　　いづこなり

ねまちづき

　　げんじのきみ

　　　　はいづこなり

季語　寝待ち月（ねまちづき、秋）

月の出が遅く寝て待つ月。厳密には陰暦8月19日の月をさすが、転じて、広く、陰暦20前後の月をさす。

Nemachi zuki

Genji no kimi wa

izuko nari

Waiting for the twentieth-night moon to rise

when will the Shining Genji

come visit me

Season word: *nemachi zuki* (*lit.*, "moon that rises while

one waits for it, lying on the bed," the twentieth-night

moon; autumn)

This moon refers to the nineteenth-night moon in August in the

traditional calendar, and also the twentieth-night moon in every

month in today's calendar. The Shining Genji is the protagonist

of *The Tale of Genji* by Lady Murasaki (970?–1013?).

神宮外苑

　　銀杏黄葉の

　　　　金屏風

じんぐうがいえん

　　いちょうもみじの

　　　　きんびょうぶ

季語　銀杏黄葉（いちょうもみじ、秋）

神宮外苑は、明治神宮外苑のこと。青山通りから明治神

宮外苑まで続く銀杏の並木道は黄葉で有名。

Jingū Gaien

　　ichō momiji no

　　　　kin byōbu

The Meiji Shrine Outer Garden

　　the golden screens of ginko-tree fall foliage

　　　　adorn the avenue

Season word: *ichō momiji* (fall foliage of ginko trees; autumn)

The avenue of the Meiji Shrine Outer Garden in Tokyo is known for the fall foliage of ginko trees.

望月や

　　栄枯盛衰

　　　　千の年

もちづきや

　　えいこせいすい

　　　　せんのとし

季語　望月（もちづき、秋）

藤原道長（966年−1027年）が、寛仁（かんにん）2年

（1018年）10月16日に詠んだ、「この世をばわが世とぞ

思ふ望月の欠けたることもなしと思へば」の歌の、千年記

念。確認すると、当日は本当に満月であった（2018年の

旧暦10月16日は、11月23日）。

Mochi zuki ya

    eiko seisui

        sen no toshi

The full moon

    the rise and fall

        of one thousand years

Season word: *mochi zuki* (the full moon; autumn)

This alludes to the poem by Fujiwara no Michinaga (966–1028),

the aristocrat and the emperor's regent of the Heian period,

written on October 16, 1018 in the traditional calendar, about the

zenith of his reign. It was confirmed that that day was in fact the

full moon. The full moon in October 2018 marks a millennium

of the poem that Michinaga wrote.

カシオペア

　　「魔笛」のアリア

　　　　絶唱す

カシオペア

　　まてきのアリア

　　　　ぜっしょうす

季語　カシオペア（カシオペア座、秋）

カシオペアはギリシア神話の女王。「夜の女王」は、モー
ツアルト（1756 年−1791 年）晩年のオペラ『魔笛』の中の
有名なアリア。

Kashiopea

Mateki no aria

zesshō su

Queen Cassiopeia

sings the aria

of the Magic Flute sublimely

Season word: *Kashiopea* (Queen Cassiopeia, the

constellation Cassiopeia; autumn)

The aria in *The Magic Flute* by W. A. Mozart (1756–1791)

is one of the two famous Queen of the Night's Arias (No.

14) in the opera. Queen Cassiopeia appears in Greek

mythology.

小春日や

　　　車椅子引く

　　　　　影長し

こはるびや

　　　くるまいすひく

　　　　　かげながし

季語　小春日（こはるび、冬）

「小春」は、陰暦 10 月の異称で、初冬の穏やかで暖かい

春のような日和をさす。

Koharu bi ya

    kuruma isu hiku

        kage nagashi

The Indian summer

    the shadow of the one pulling the wheel chair

        is long and thin

Season word: *ko haru bi (lit.*, "little spring day" refers to a fine warm day in October in the traditional calendar, which corresponds to late October–late December today; winter)

Winter in the lunar calendar ran from October to December.

November

Photograph 11. Winter sky with migrating birds.

嬬恋の

　　白根の山に

　　　　霜の降る

つまごいの

　　しらねのやまに

　　　　しものふる

季語　霜（しも、冬）

嬬恋村は、群馬県吾妻（あがつま）郡にあり、本白根山（もとしらねさん）や万座（まんざ）温泉などがある。

Tsumagoi no

    Shirane no yama ni

        shimo no furu

In Tsumagoi

    the frost is forming

        on Mt. Shirane

Season word: *shimo* (frost; winter)

Tsumagoi is a village in Agatsuma county, Gunma prefecture. Surrounded by mountains, it is part of the Jōshin'etsu-kōgen National Park and is the location of the Manza hot spring.

224

初時雨

　　　薔薇の根の聴く

　　　　子守唄

はつしぐれ

　　　ばらのねのきく

　　　　こもりうた

季語　初時雨（はつしぐれ、冬）

Hatsu shigure

baba no ne no kiku

komori uta

The first drizzle

the root of rose bush listens to it

like a lullaby

Season word: *hatsu shigure* (first winter drizzle of the

season; winter)

薔薇窓や

　　千の硝子に

　　　　千の霜

ばらまどや

　　せんのガラスに

　　　　せんのしも

季語　霜(しも、冬)

227

Bara mado ya

sen no garasu ni

sen no shimo

The rose window is adorned

with thousands of glass pieces

and thousands of frost pieces

Season word: *shimo* (frost; winter)

月冴ゆる

　　　最期の一葉

　　　　　不動なり

つきさゆる

　　　さいごのひとは

　　　　　ふどうなり

季語　　月冴ゆる(つきさゆる、冬)

オー・ヘンリー(1862年–1910年)の『最後の一葉』へのオ
マージュ。

Tsuki sayuru

    saigo no hitoha

        fudō nari

The cold, crisp moon

    the last leaf

        stays put

Season word: *sayuru sora* (a cold, crisp moon; winter)

This is a homage to *The Last Leaf* by O. Henry (1862–1910).

凍窓に映ゆ

　　　下弦の月の

　　　　　いと美しき

いてまどにはゆ

　　　かげんのつきの

　　　　　いとはしき

季語　凍窓（いてまど、冬）

下弦の月は、残月（満月の後の月）の半月のこと。

Ite mado ni hayu

kagen no tsuki no

ito hashi ki

The last quarter moon

reflected on the freezing window

is very pretty

Season word: *ite mado* (freezing window; winter)

冬夕焼

　　山里の鳥

　　　　不死鳥のごと

ふゆゆやけ

　　やまざとのとり

　　　　ふしちょうのごと

季語　冬夕焼（ふゆゆやけ、冬）

Fuyu yuyake

    yama zaso no tori

        fushichō no goto

The winter sunset glory

    the bird in the mountain field

        shines like a phoenix

Season word: *fuyu yuyake* (a winter sunset glory; winter)

鉛空

　　背負ひて寒し

　　　　姨捨山

なまりぞら

　　せおいてさむし

　　　　おばすてやま

季語　寒し(寒い、さむい、冬)

Namari zora

seoi te samushi

Obasute yama

Carrying the lead-like sky

on its shoulder

Mt. Obasute is cold

Season word: *samushi* (it is cold; winter)

Mt. Obasute (*lit.*, "a mountain to dump grandmothers")

refers to a mountain to which elderly women were taken

and left to freeze to death. This was a tradition of poor

mountain villages in Japan when elderly people were no

longer able to work on the farm and became a burden on

the family.

雪あられ

　　　　大地を弾き

　　　　　胸弾く

ゆきあられ

　　　　だいちをはじき

　　　　　むねはじく

季語　雪あられ（ゆきあられ、冬）

Yuki arare

    daichi o hajiki

        mune hajiku

The snow hail

    bounces the earth

        and the heart of the child

Season word: *yuki arare* (snow hail; winter)

冬北斗

　　　母のふらhere

　　　　跳ぶ子熊

ふゆほくと

　　　ははのふらここ

　　　　とぶこぐま

季語　冬北斗（ふゆほくと、冬の北斗七星、おおぐま座、
冬）

「ふらここ」は、ブランコの雅語。北斗七星（おおぐま座）を
ブランコに見立てる。北斗七星は、こぐま座と一緒に毎日、
北天を回る。

239

Fuyu hokuto

    haha no furakoko

      tobu ko guma

The Big Dipper

    the Little Bear jumps

      on his mother's swing

Season word: *fuyu hokuto* (The Big Dipper in the winter; winter)

The Big Dipper, made of seven bright stars of the constellation Ursa Major (the Big Bear), circles around Polaris, the North Star in the Little Dipper, the constellation Ursa Minor.

オリオンや

　　ギリシャ神話の

　　　　シンフォニー

オリオンや

　　ギリシャしんわの

　　　　シンフォニー

季語　オリオン（オリオン座、冬）

ギリシャ神話には、オリオンにまつわる話が多くある。

Orion ya

    Girishia shinwa no

       shinphonii

The constellation Orion

    the symphonies

       of Greek mythology

Season word: *Orion* (the constellation Orion; winter)

December

Photograph 12. Winter sky with a pearl-like sun.

富士の嶺

　　五つの湖に

　　　　冬を撒く

ふじのみね

　　いつつのうみに

　　　　ふゆをまく

季語　冬（ふゆ、冬）

「五つの湖」は、富士五湖をさす。

Fuji no mine

    itsutsu no umi ni

       fuyu o maku

The summit of Mt. Fuji

    is scattering winter

       to the five lakes

Season word: *fuyu* (winter; winter)

The "five lakes" refers to the Fuji Five Lakes.

雪原や

　　無常の世界

　　　　果てし無く

せつげんや

　　むじょうのせかい

　　　　はてしなく

季語　雪原（せつげん、冬）

Setsu gen ya

mujō no sekai

hateshi naku

The snow field

the world of evanescence

spreads endlessly

Season word: *sestsu gen* (snow field; winter)

凩や

　　　星啼く空と

　　　　　啼く湖と

こがらしや

　　　ほしなくそらと

　　　　　なくうみと

季語　凩（木枯し、こがらし、冬）

Kogarashi ya

    hoshi naku sora to

      naku umi to

The wintry wind

    the star sobs in the sky

      and the lake sobs

Season word: *kogarashi* (wintry wind; winter)

冬空や

　　真珠を飾る

　　　　燻し銀

ふゆぞらや

　　しんじゅをかざる

　　　　いぶしぎん

季語　冬空（ふゆぞら、冬）

冬の日、燻し銀のような鈍色の雲に太陽が真珠のように輝く様子。

Fuyu zora ya

    shinju o kazaru

      ibushi gin

The winter sky

    the pearl-like sun

      adorns the oxidized-silver sky

Season word: *fuyu zora* (winter sky; winter)

The clouds in the winter sky look like oxidized silver,

while the sun looks like a pearl.

雪の夜は

　　　誰かに遭へる

　　　　　気配せり

ゆきのよは

　　　だれかにあえる

　　　　　けはいせり

季語　雪の夜（ゆきのよ、冬）

Yuki no yo wa

    dare ka ni aeru

        kehai seri

The snowy night

    one anticipates

        someone might come to visit

Season word: *yuki no yo* (snowy night; winter)

白川郷

　　　合掌唱ふ

　　　　　豪雪の里

しらかわごう

　　　がっしょうとなう

　　　　　ごうせつのさと

季語　　豪雪(ごうせつ、冬)

岐阜県、白川郷の合掌造りは、ユネスコ世界文化遺産に

登録される。

「唱ふ」は、唱えるの文語体。

Shirakawa gō

gasshō tonau

gōsetsu no sato

Shirakawa village

the chanting prayers reverberate

in the village of heavy snow

Season word: *gōsetsu* (extremely heavy snow; winter)

Shirakawa village, Gifu prefecture, is known for its

architectural style of houses specifically designed to cope

with heavy snow. It is called *gasshō zukuri*, because it

resembles the posture of *gasshō* (of prayer putting the

hands together).

粉雪や

　　真白き影の

　　　　付き纏ふ

こなゆきや

　　ましろきかげの

　　　　つきまとう

季語　粉雪（こなゆき、冬）

Kona yuki ya

    ma shikoki kage no

        tsuki matou

The power snow

    one feels as if

        the pure white shadow is following

Season word: *kona yuki* (power snow; winter)

雪女

　　　黄泉へ誘ふ

　　　　　微笑なり

ゆきおんな

　　　よみへいざなう

　　　　　びしょうなり

季語　雪女（ゆきおんな、冬）

Yuki on'na

yomi e izanau

bishō nairi

The snow woman

her icy smile lures one

to the world of the dead

Season word: *yuki on'na* (the snow woman; winter)

The snow woman is an imaginary mystical creature in

Japanese folklore.

冴へ月や

　　肌刺す光

　　　　冴へ返す

さえつきや

　　はださすひかり

　　　　さえかえす

季語　冴へ月（さえつき、冬）

261

Sae tsuki ya

hada sasu hikari

sae kaesu

The piercing cold moon

the light piercing the skin

is reflecting back to the moon

Season word: *sae tsuki* (a piercing cold moon; winter)

天狼星

　　天の海原

　　　　永遠の旅

てんろうせい

　　　てんのうなばら

　　　　とわのたび

季語　天狼星（てんろうせい、シリウス、冬）

シリウスは、おおいぬ座のアルファ星。

Tenorō sei

ten no unabara

towa no tabi

Sirius

runs around the ocean of the heavens

on an eternal voyage

Season word: *Tenorō sei* (*lit.*, "celestial wolf" refers to

Sirius; winter)

Sirius is the alpha star in the constellation Canis Major and

is known as the "Dog Star."

About the Author

Mayumi Itoh is a former Professor of Political Science at the University of Nevada, Las Vegas (UNLV). She has previously taught at Princeton University and Queens College, City University of New York (CUNY), and has written numerous books and academic journal articles. Her single-authored book titles include:

–*Globalization of Japan: Japanese Sakoku Mentality and U.S. Efforts to Open Japan* (1998)

–*The Hatoyama Dynasty: Japanese Political Leadership Through the Generations* (2003)

–*Japanese War Orphans in Manchuria: Forgotten Victims of World War II* (2010)

–*Japanese Wartime Zoo Policy: The Silent Victims of World War II* (2010)

–*The Origin of Ping-Pong Diplomacy: The Forgotten Architect of Sino-U.S. Rapprochement* (2011)

–Pioneers of Sino-Japanese Relations: Liao and Takasaki (2012)

–Hachi: The Truth of the Life and Legend of the Most Famous Dog in Japan (2013)

–The Origins of Contemporary Sino-Japanese Relations: Zhou Enlai and Japan (2016)

–The Making of China's War with Japan: Zhou Enlai and Zhang Xueliang (2016)

–The Making of China's Peace with Japan: What Xi Jinping Should Learn from Zhou Enlai (2017)

–"Hachi-ko" in Siberia: The True Story of Japanese Prisoners of War and a Dog (2017)

–Hachiko: Solving Twenty Mysteries about the Most Famous Dog in Japan (2017)

–Eliza Ruhamah Scidmore and Japan: The Life and Journeys to the Far East of the American Woman Who Brought "Sakura" to Washington, D.C. (2017)

–Kaneko Misuzu: Life and Poems of A Lonely Princess (2018)

–The Japanese Culture of Mourning Whales: Whale Graves and Memorial Monuments in Japan (2018)

–Animals and the Fukushima Nuclear Disaster (2018)

–Haikus of All Seasons I: The Heavens and the Earth (2018)

–Haikus of All Seasons II: Humanity (2018)

–Haikus of All Seasons III: Fauna (2018)

–Haikus of All Seasons IV: Flora (2018)

–Haikus of All Seasons V: The Heavens and the Earth (2018)

–Haikus of All Seasons VI: Humanity (2018)

–Haikus of All Seasons VII: Fauna (2018)

–Haikus of All Seasons VIII: Flora (2018)

–Poems of Kaneko Misuzu and Haikus Inspired by Them: Humanity (2019)

–Haikus by Princetonian: 2018–2019, ed. (2019)

–Haikus on Bald Eagles (2019)

www.ingramcontent.com/pod-product-compliance
Lightning Source LLC
Chambersburg PA
CBHW020314290526
45785CB00007B/2787